What is

Bullshit

The vulgar and Delightful Adult Coloring Book

By

S.B. Nozaz

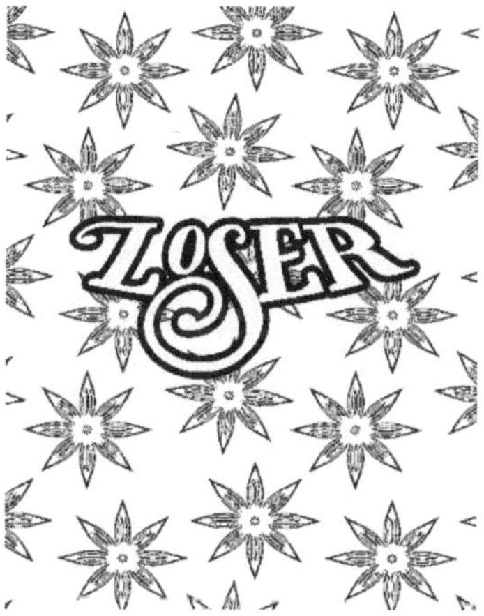

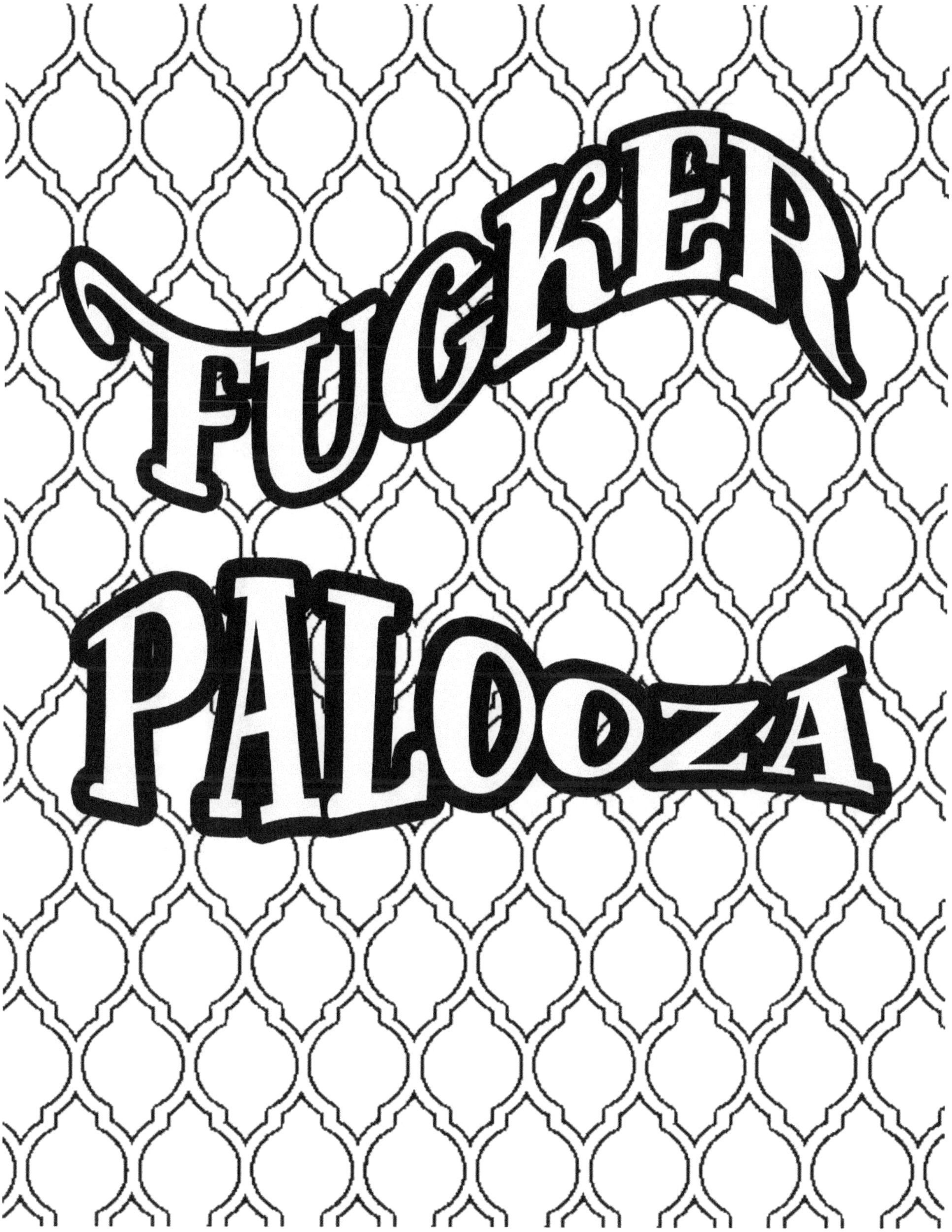
FUCKER
PALOOZA

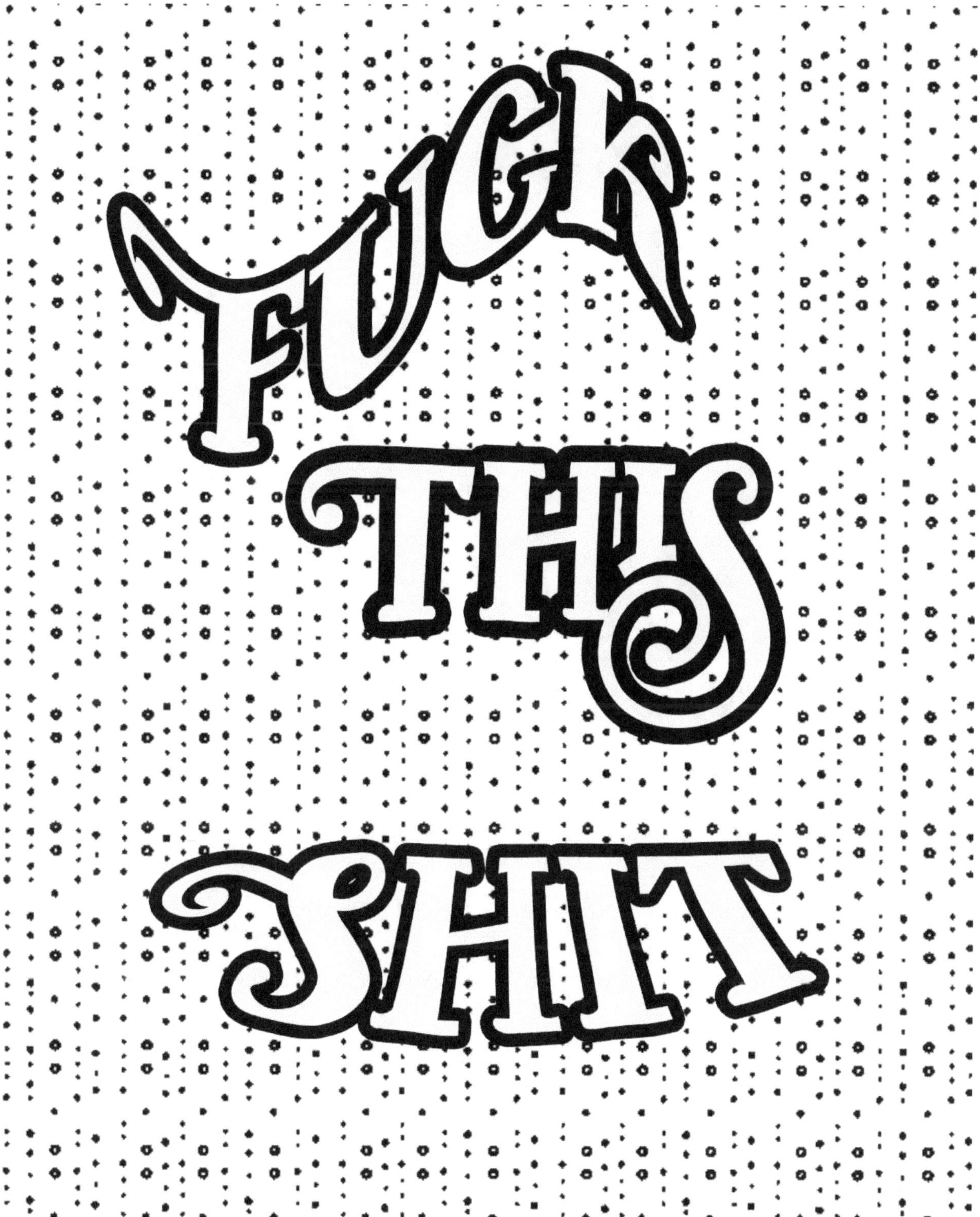
FUCK
THIS
SHIT

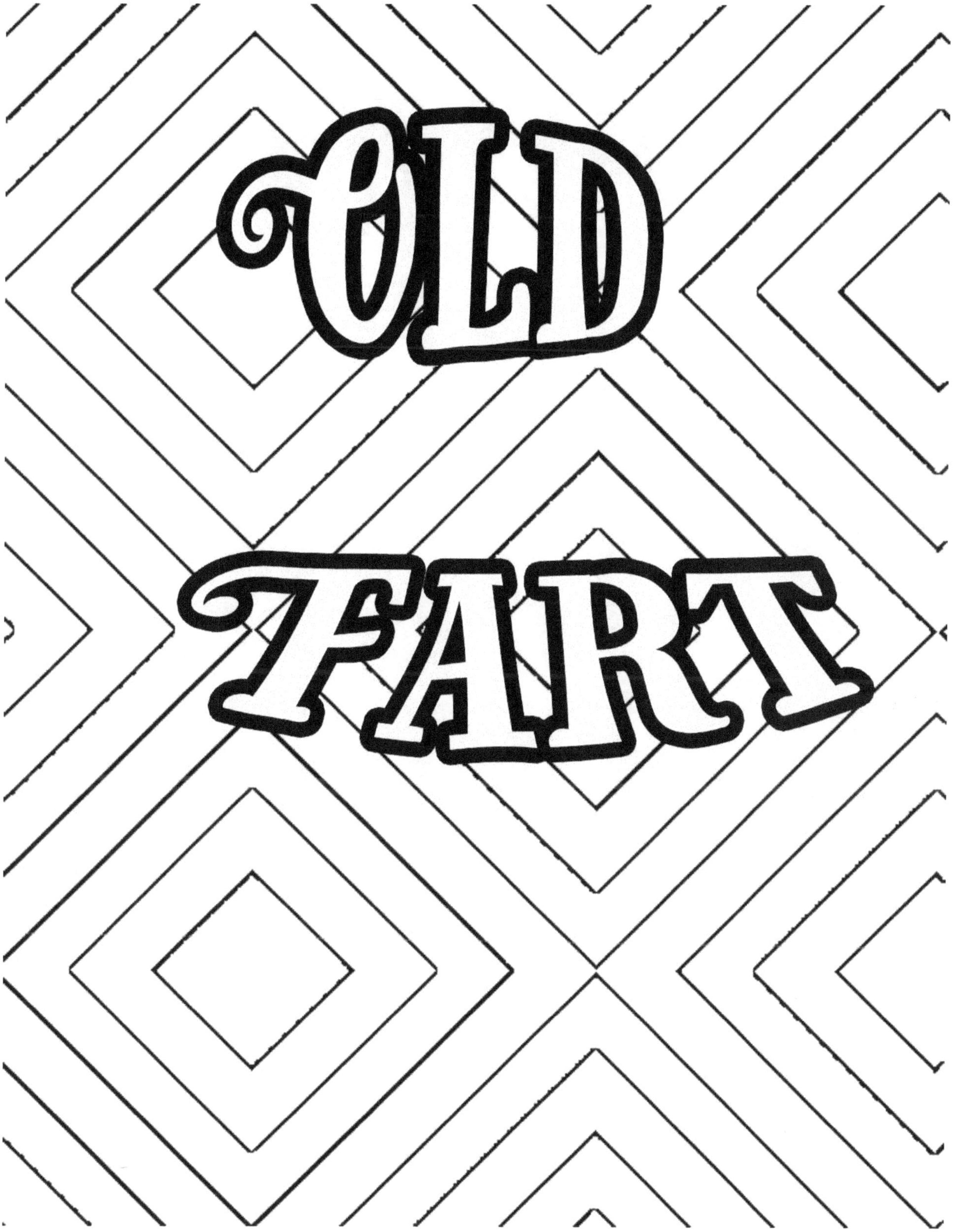
OLD
FART

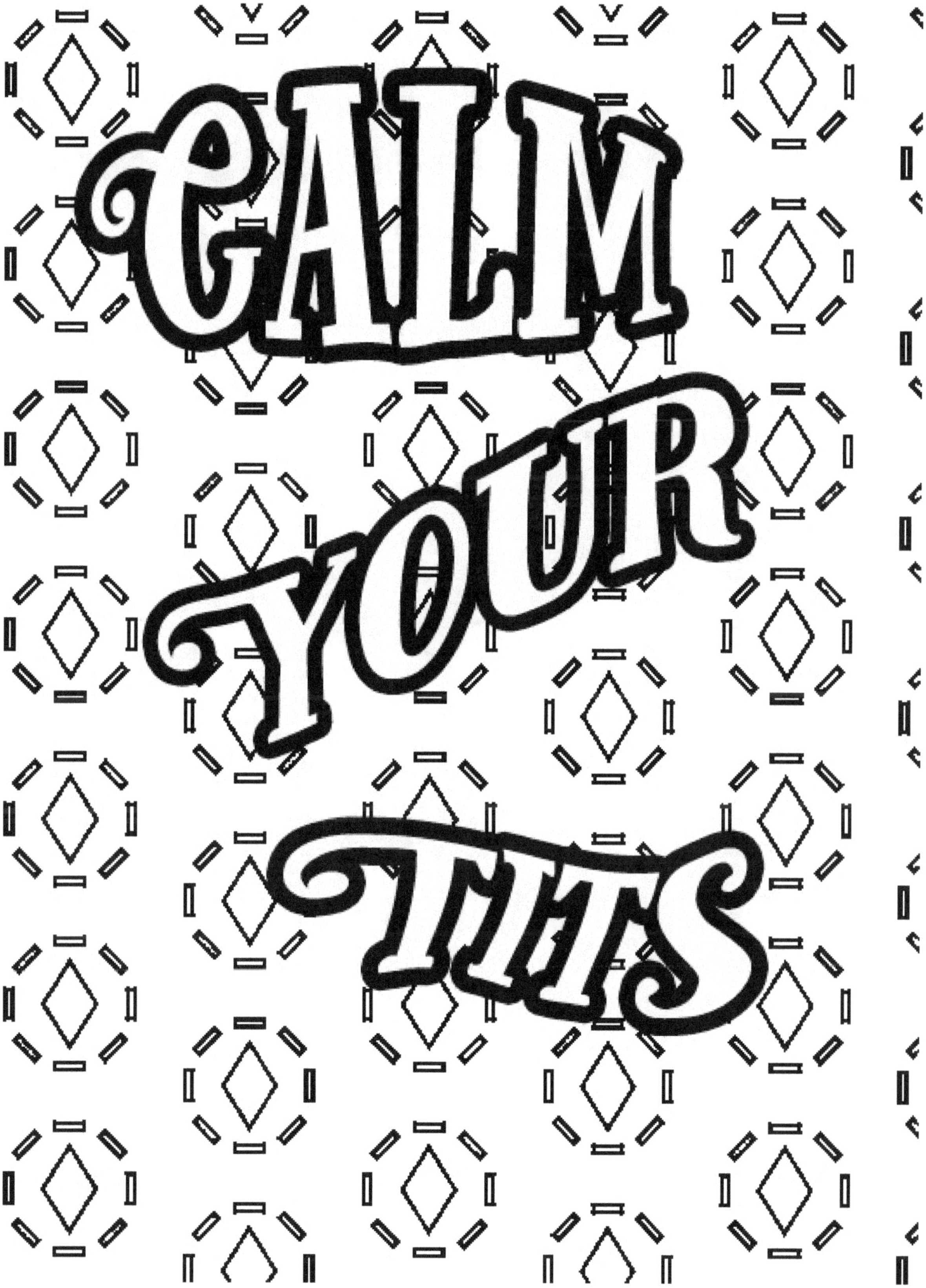
CALM
YOUR
TITS

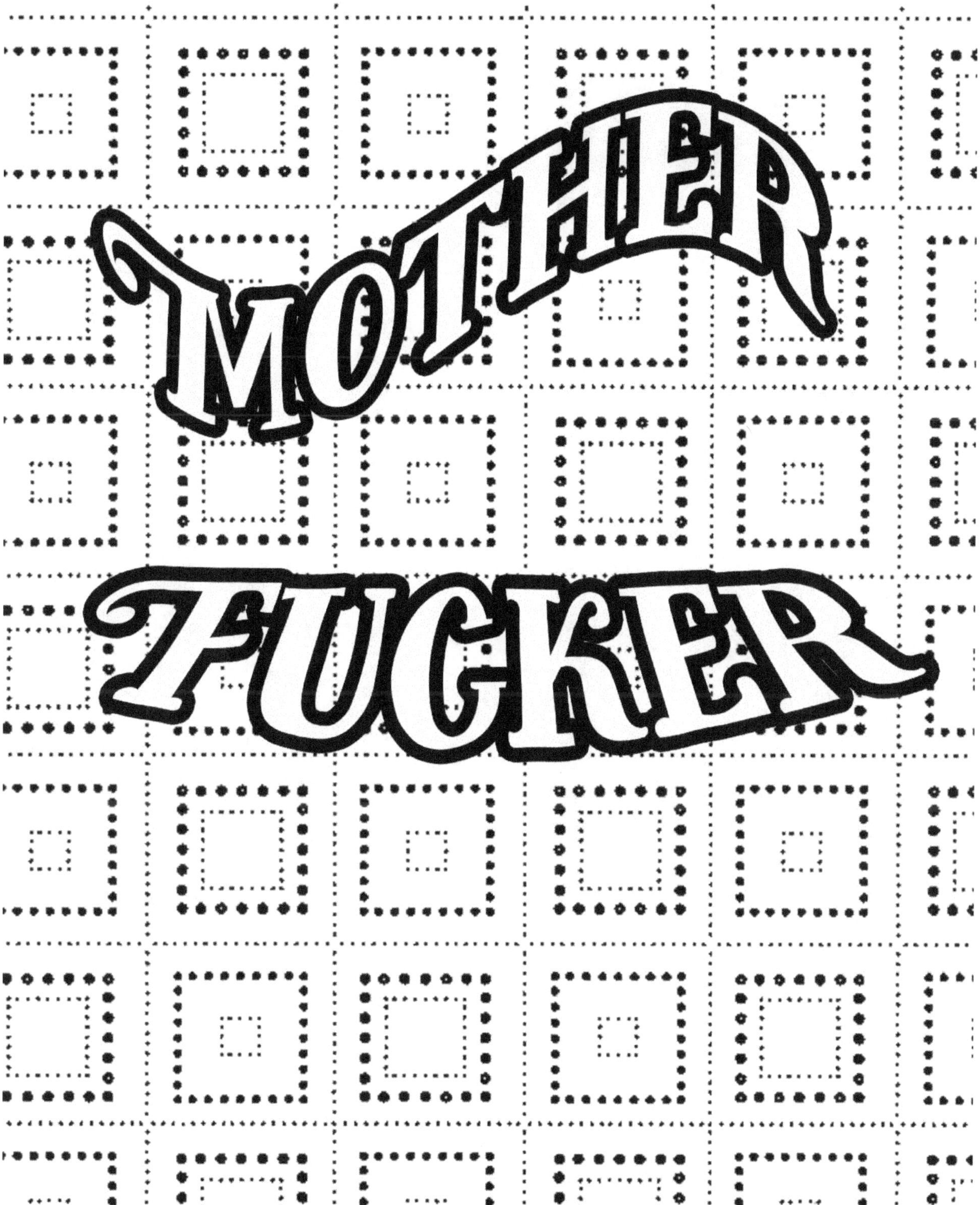
MOTHER
FUCKER

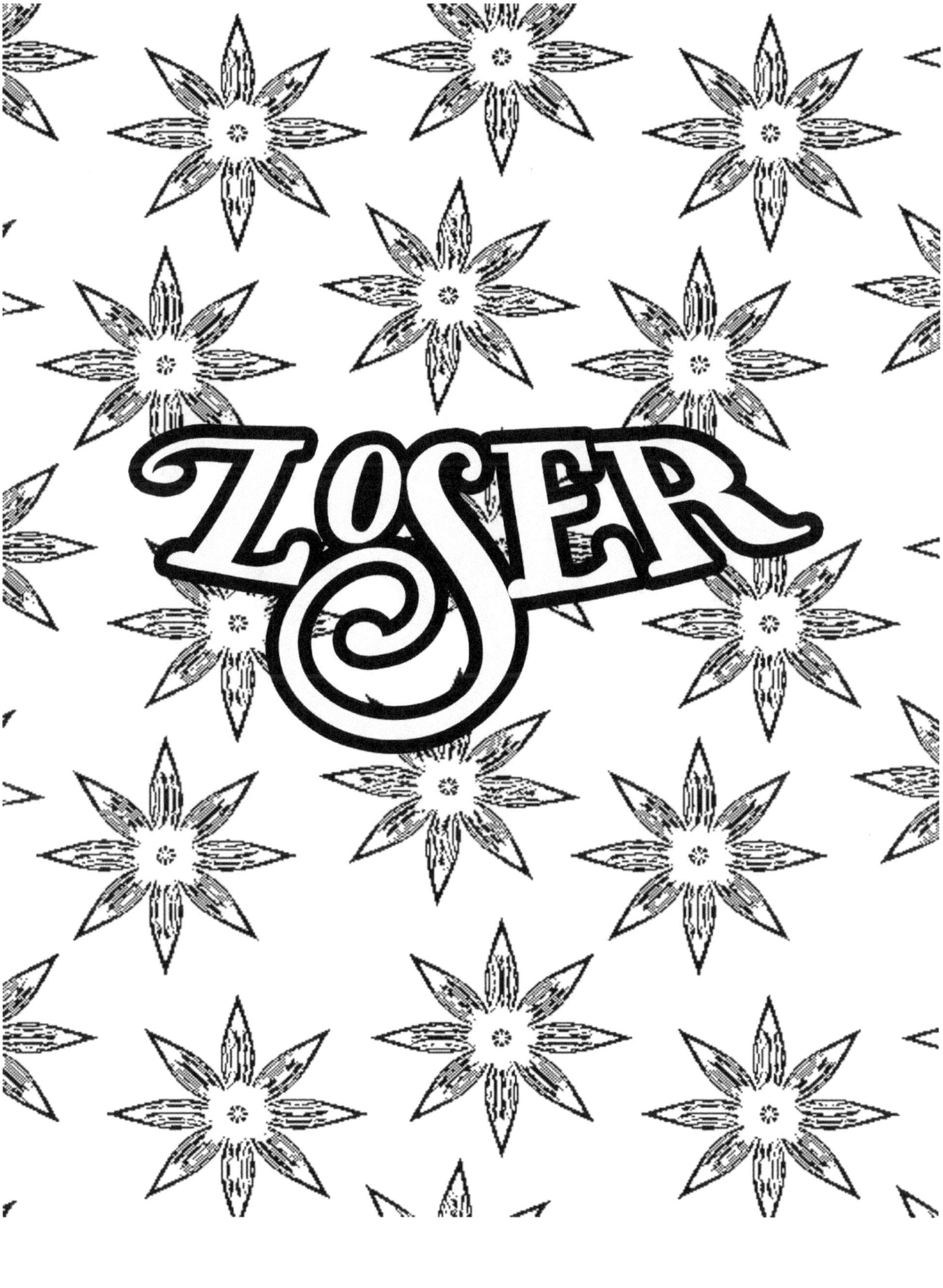
LOSER

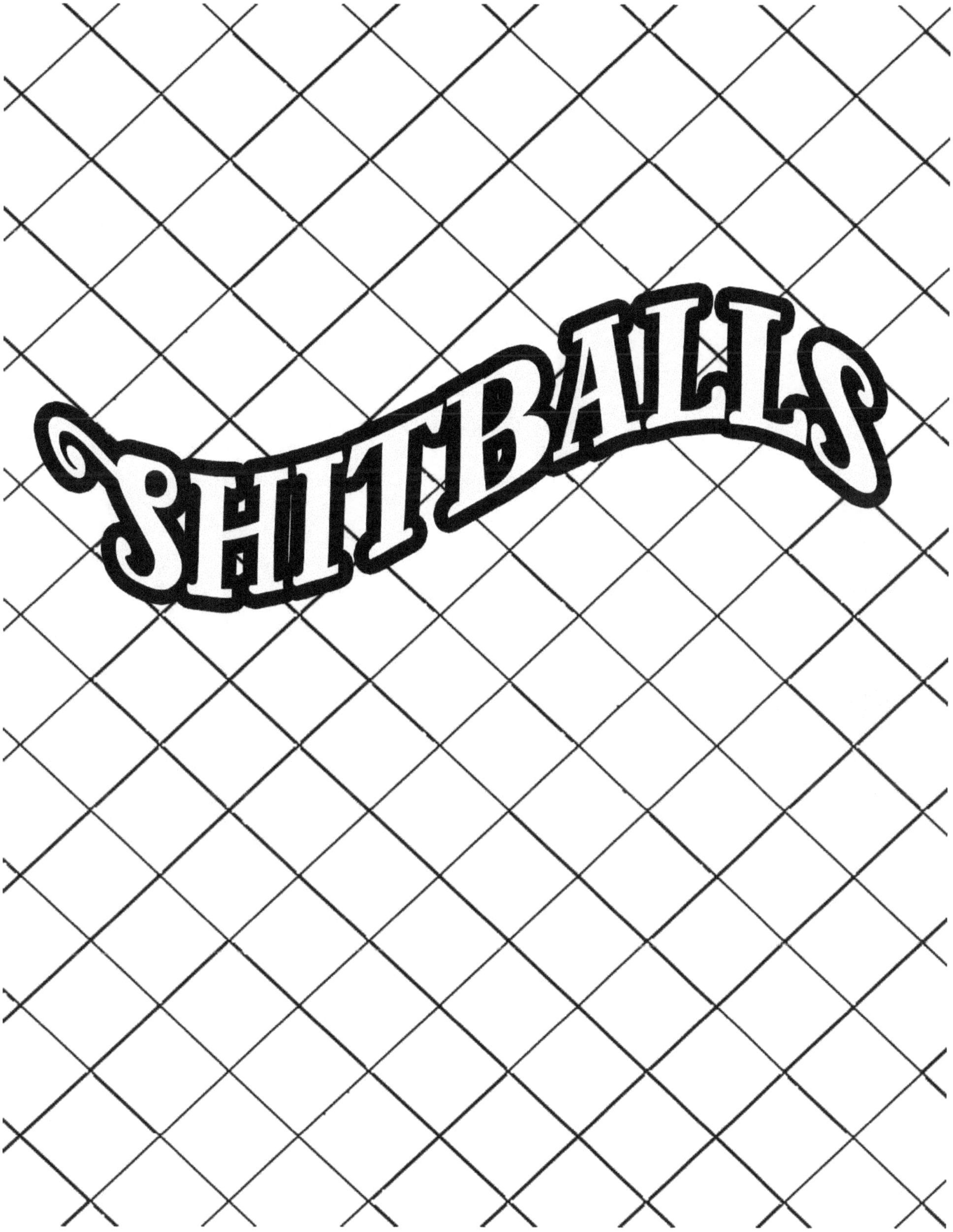
SHITBALLS

SHITFACED

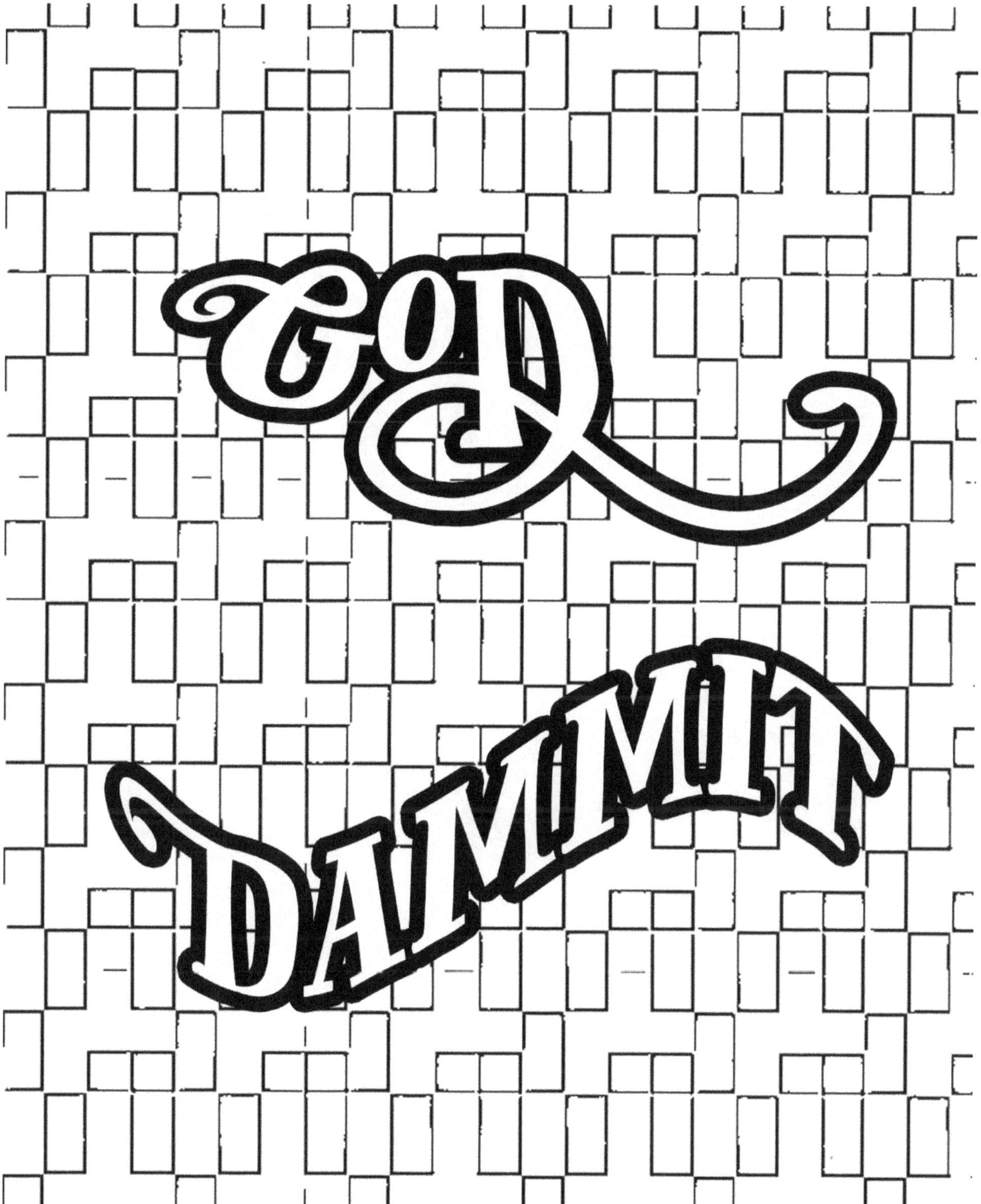
GOD
DAMMIT

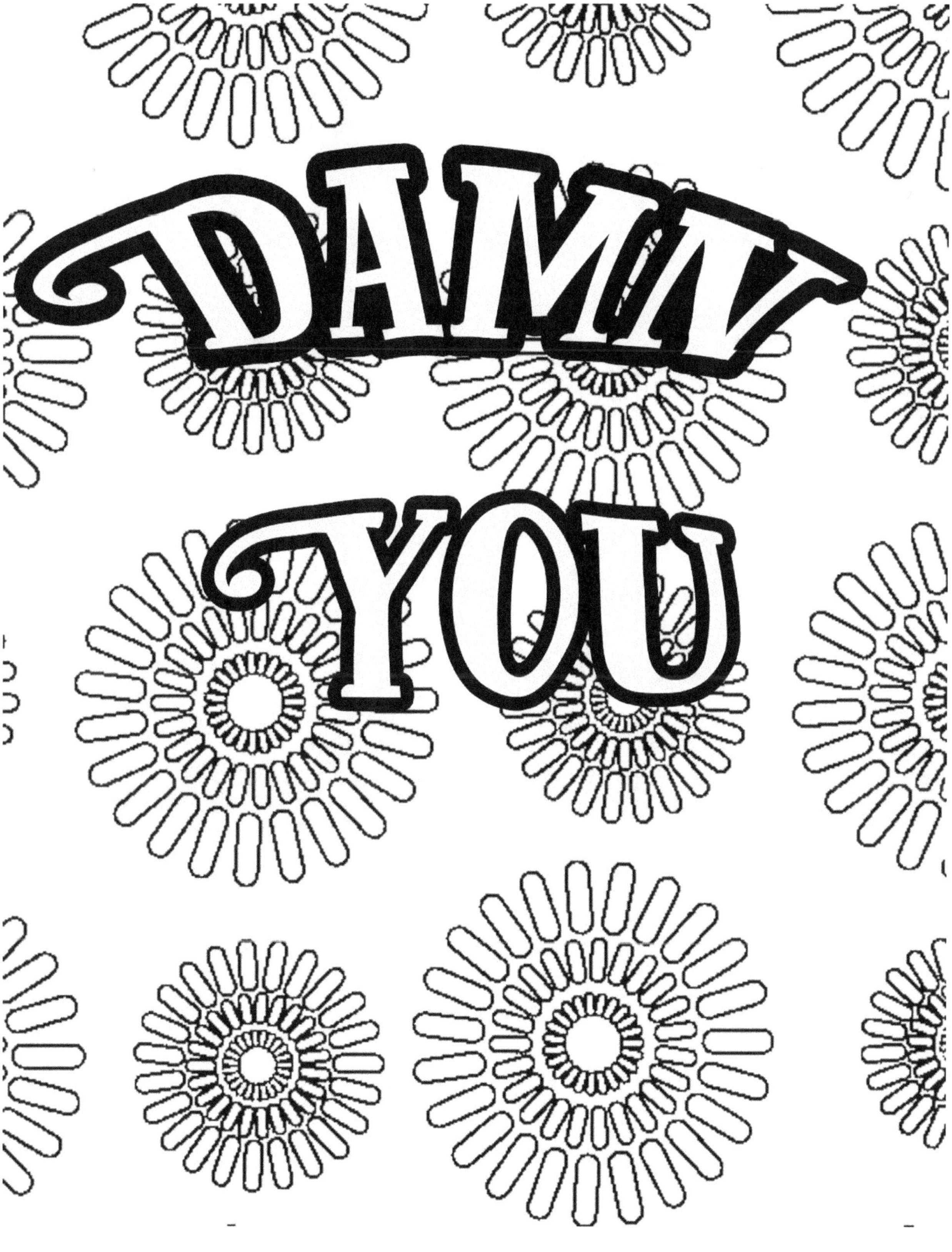
DAMN
YOU

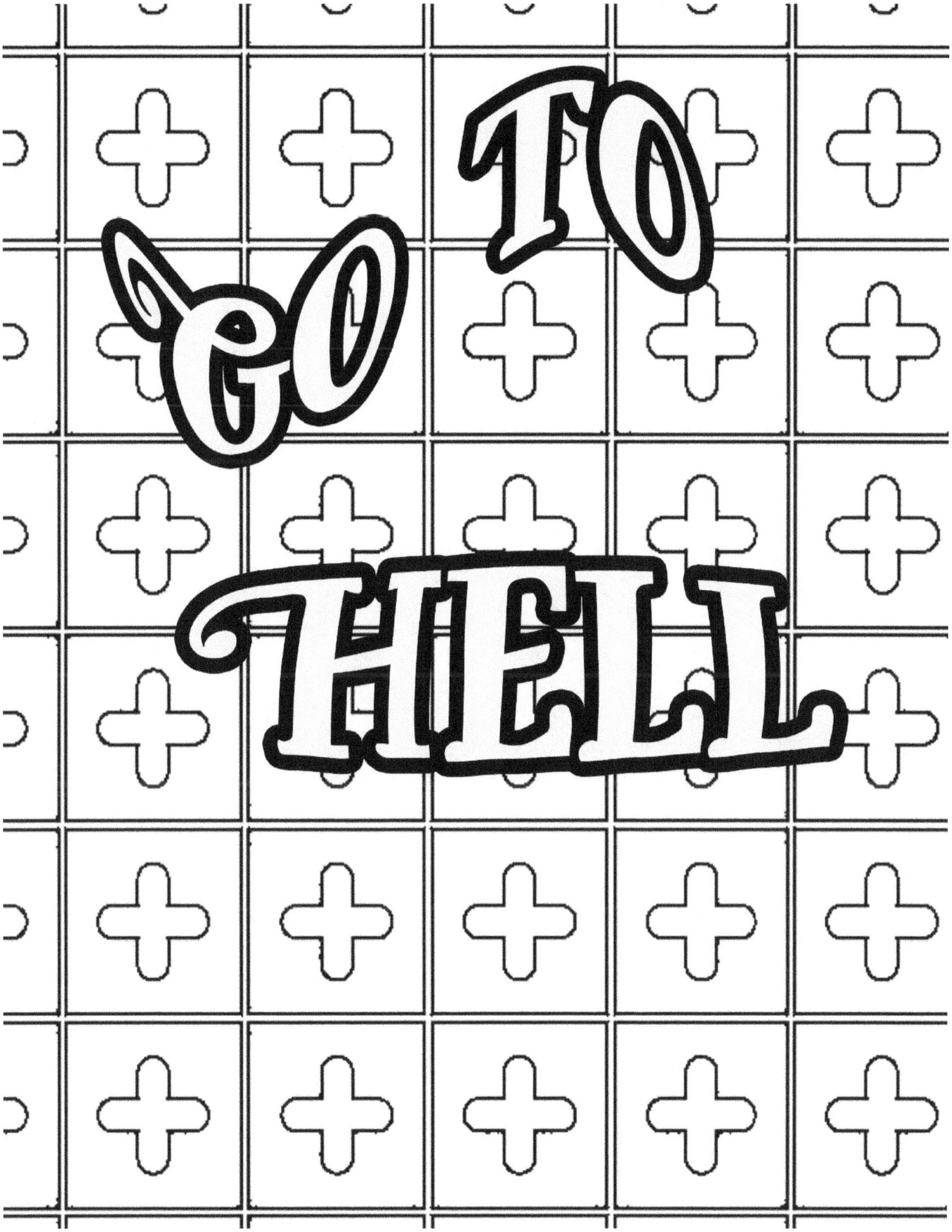
GO TO
HELL

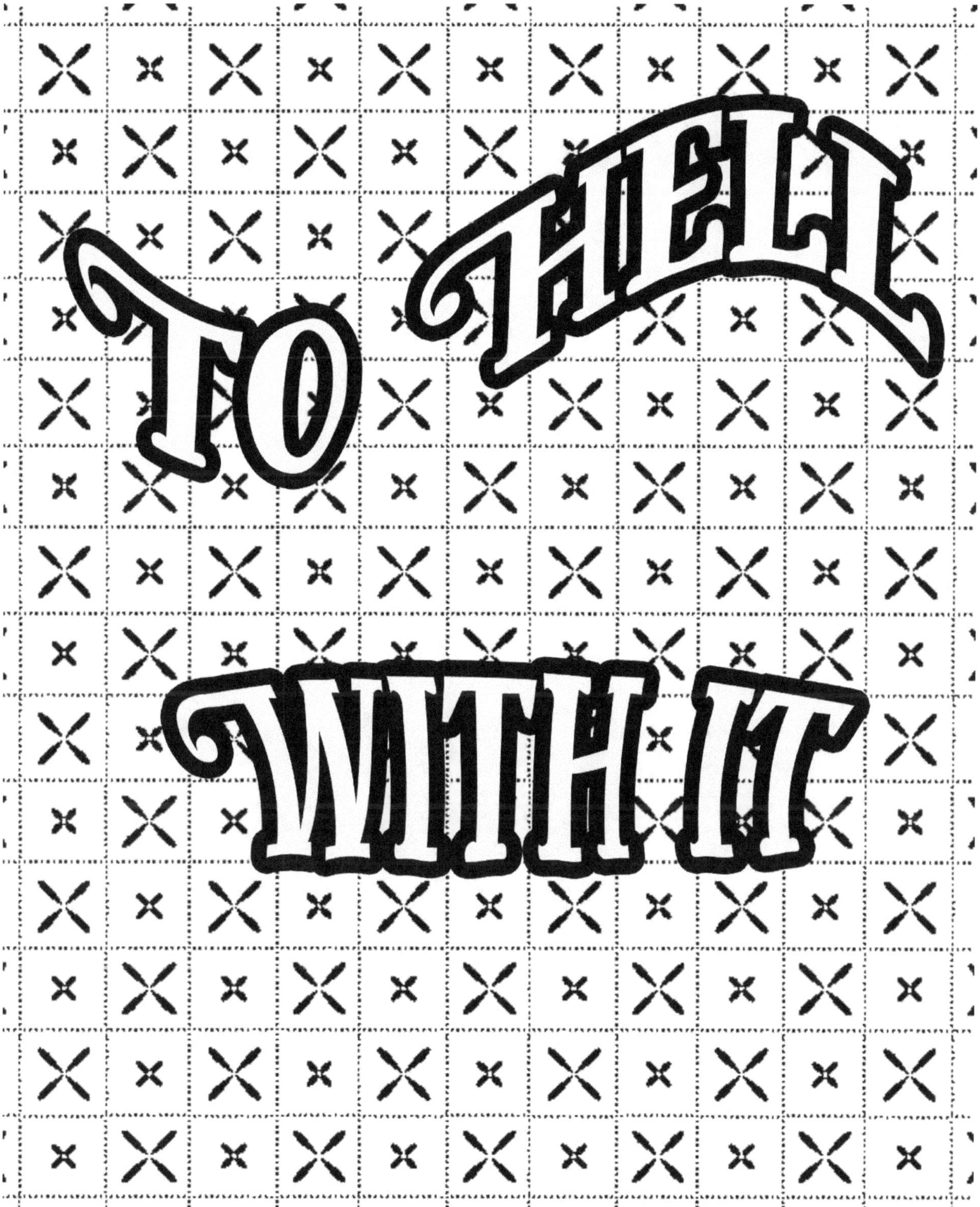
TO HELL
WITH IT

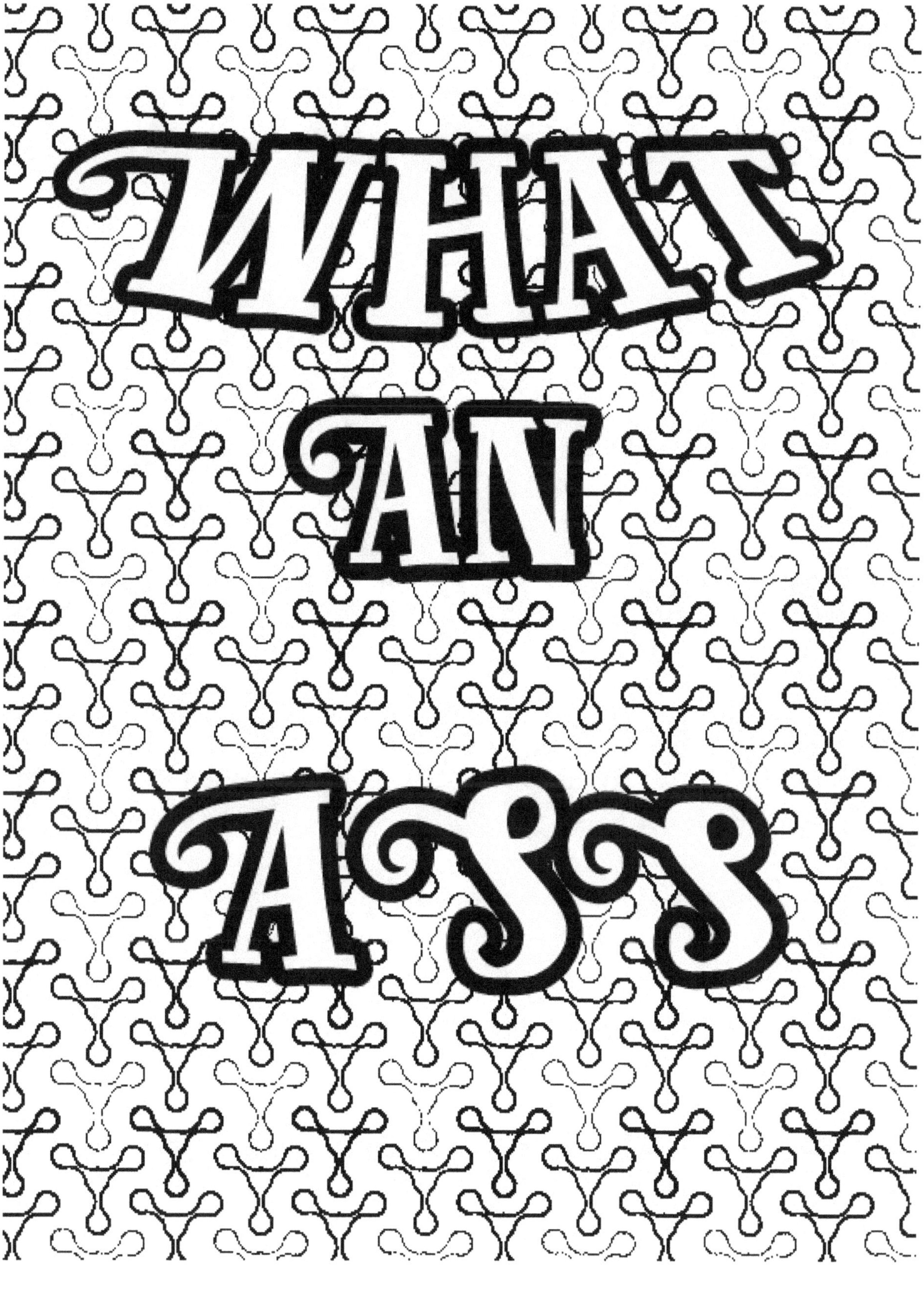
WHAT
AN
ASS

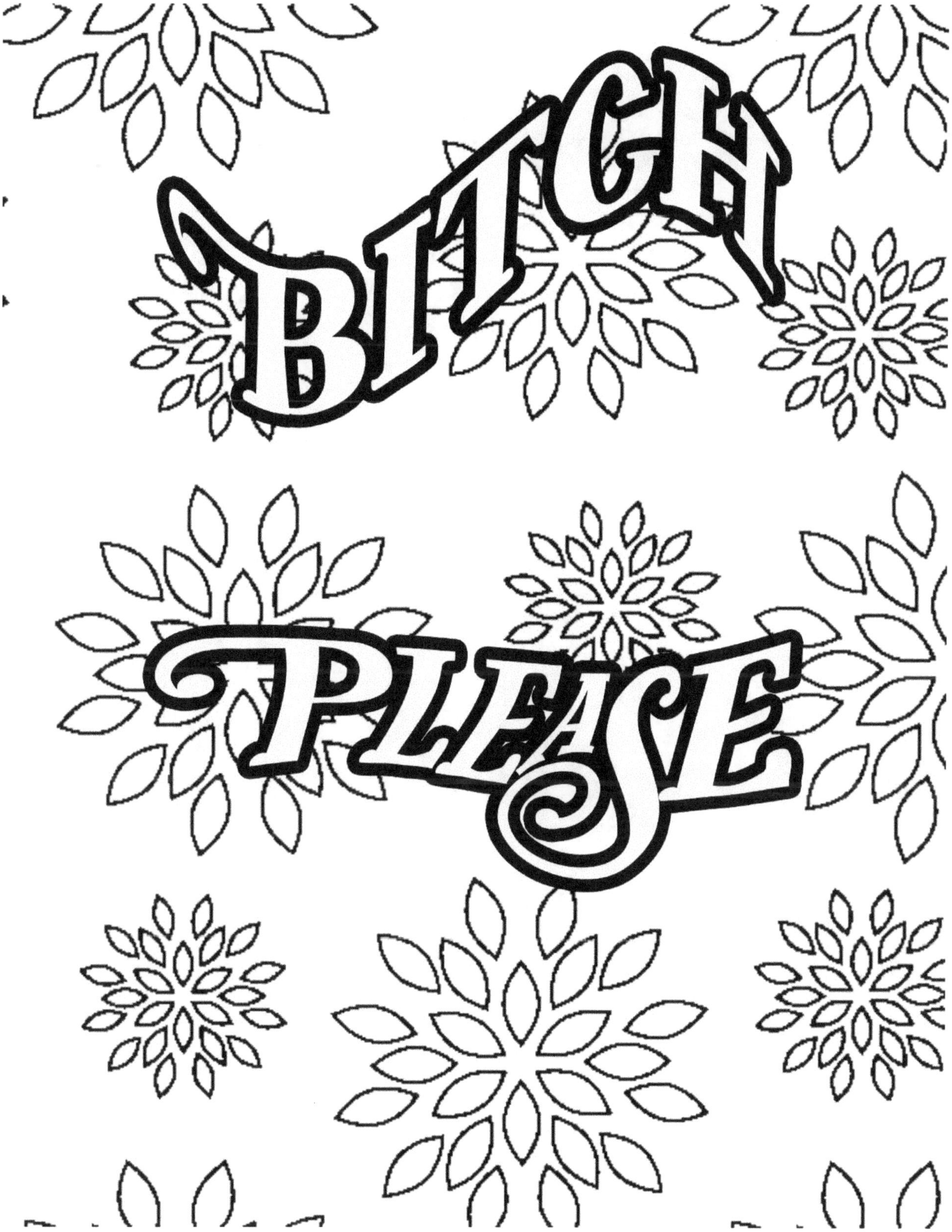
BITCH
PLEASE

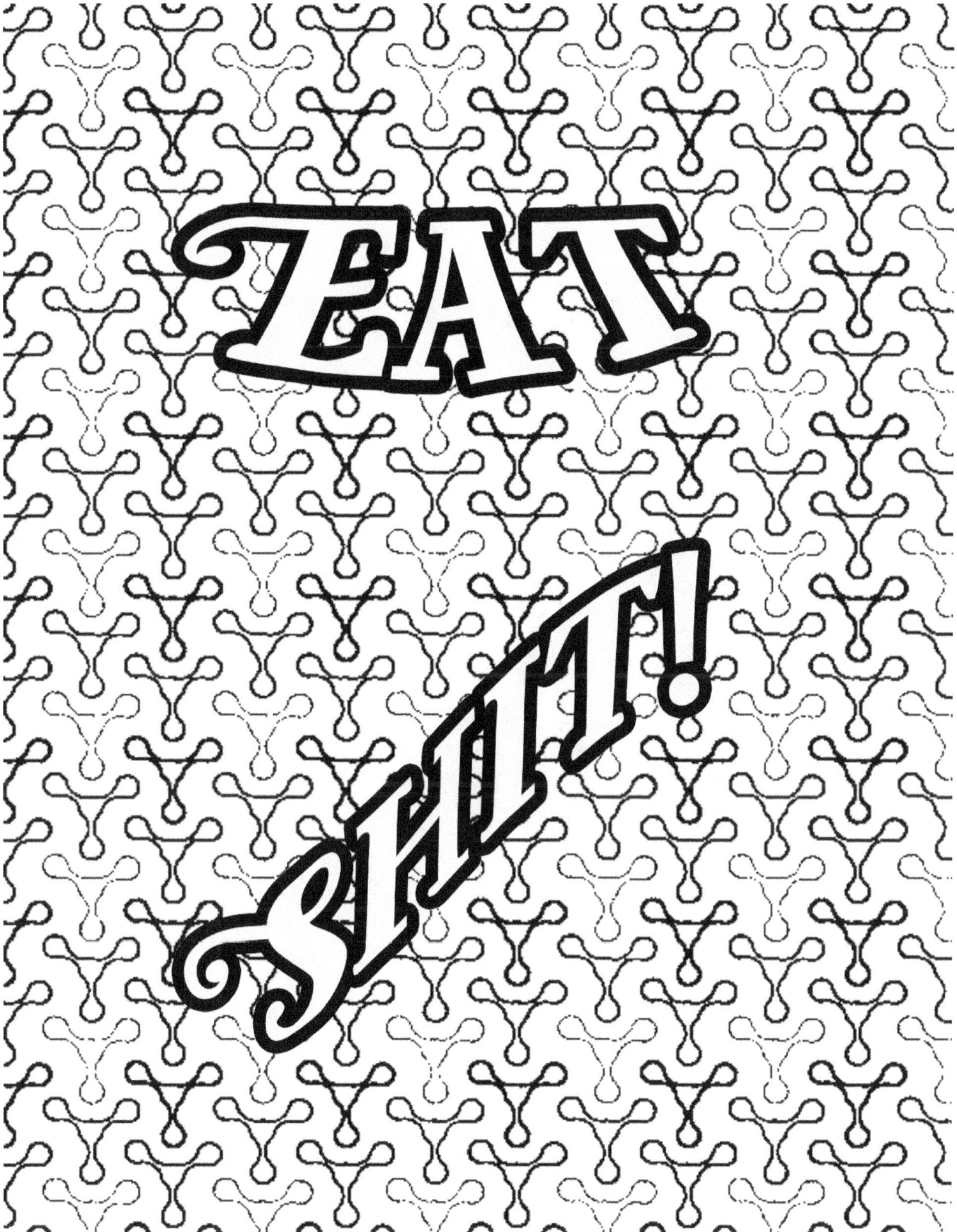
EAT
SHIT!

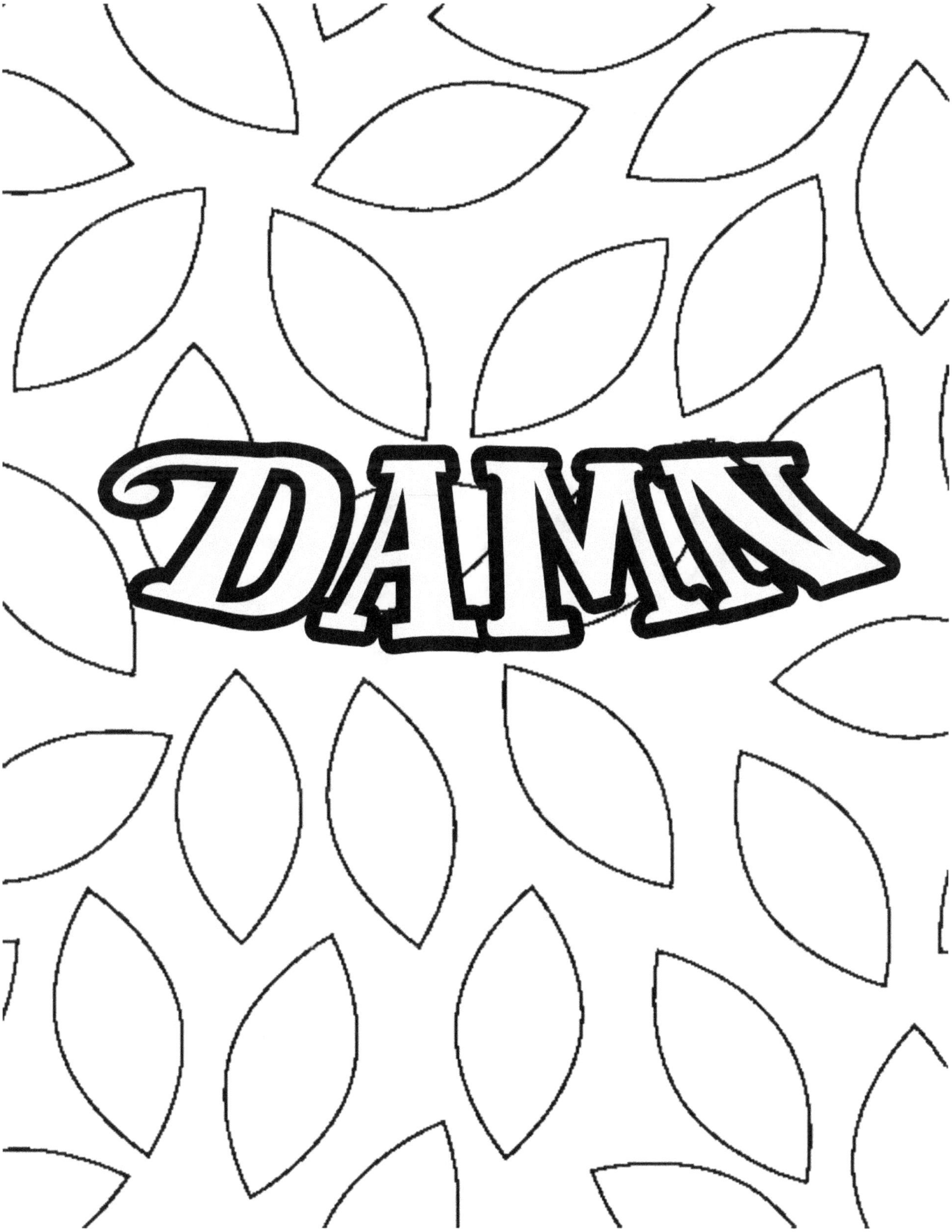
DAMN

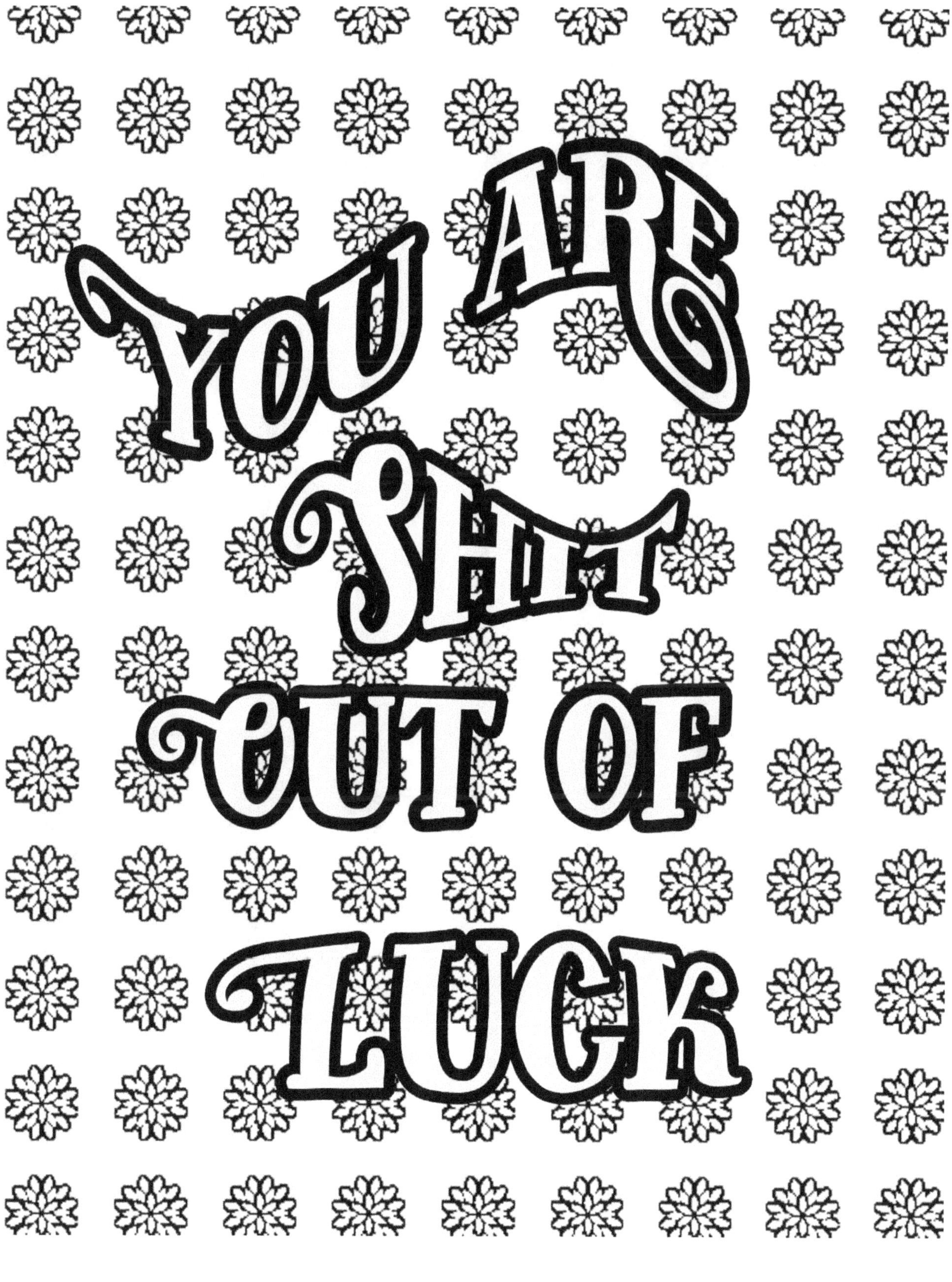
YOU ARE
SHIT
OUT OF
LUCK

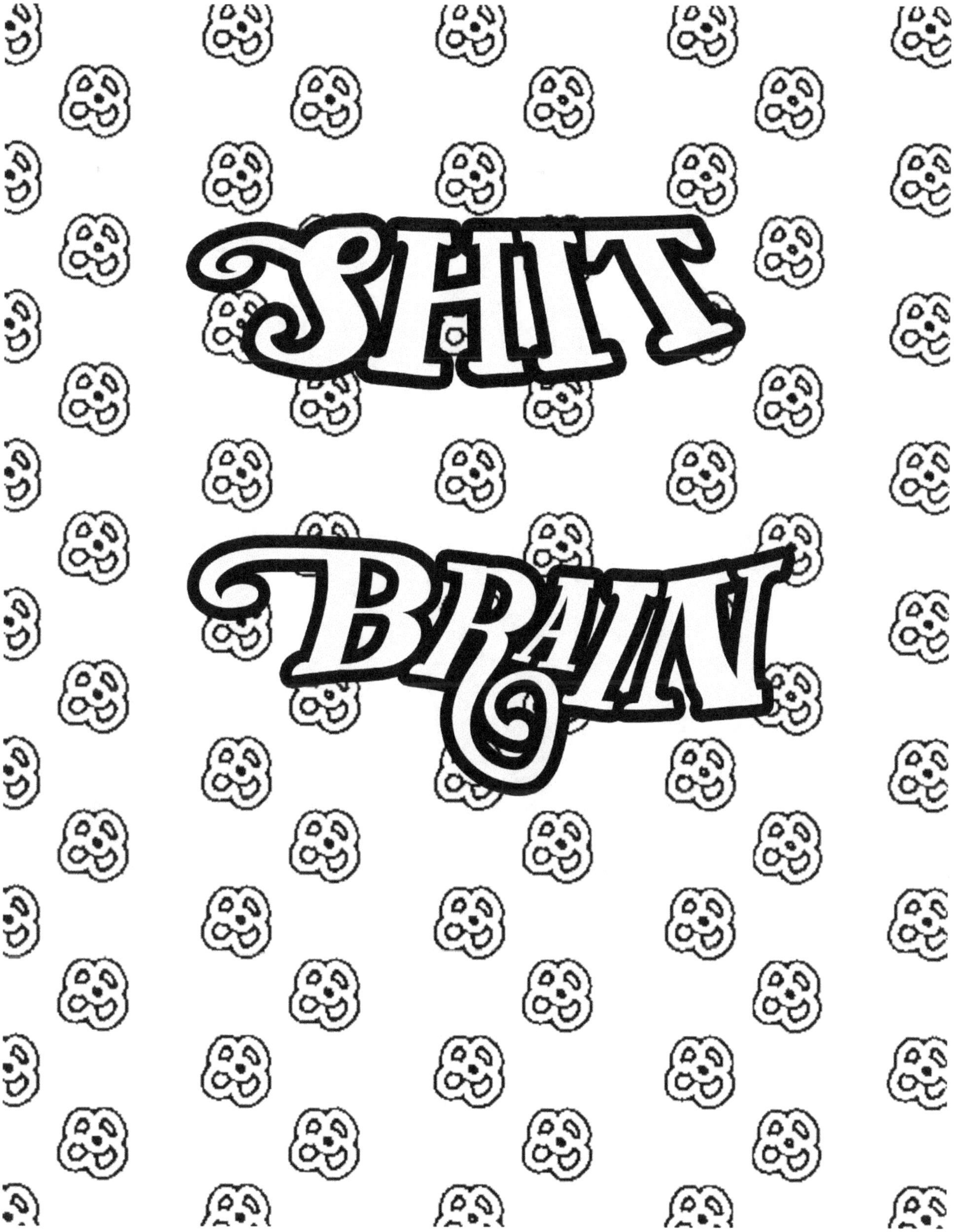
SHIT
BRAIN

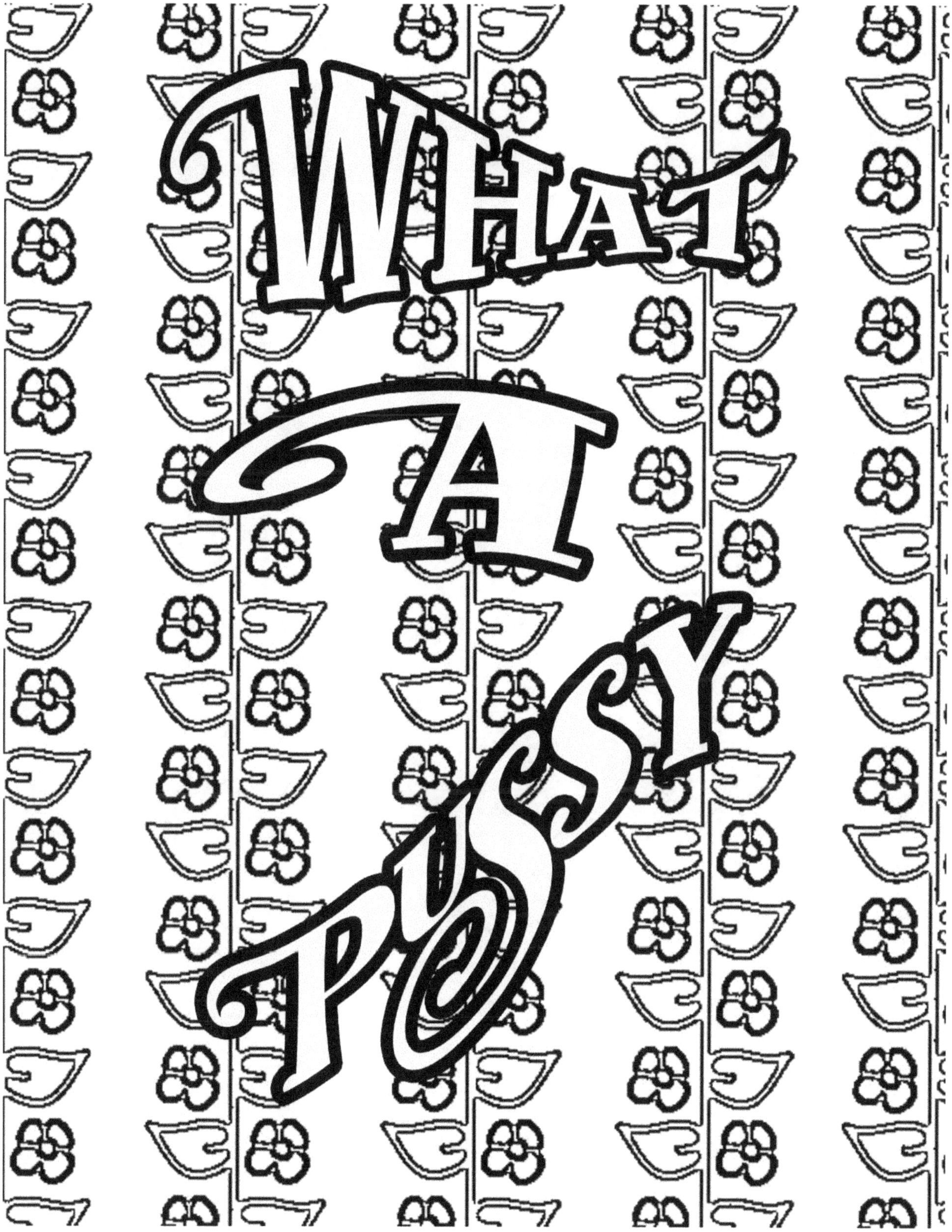
WHAT
A
PUSSY

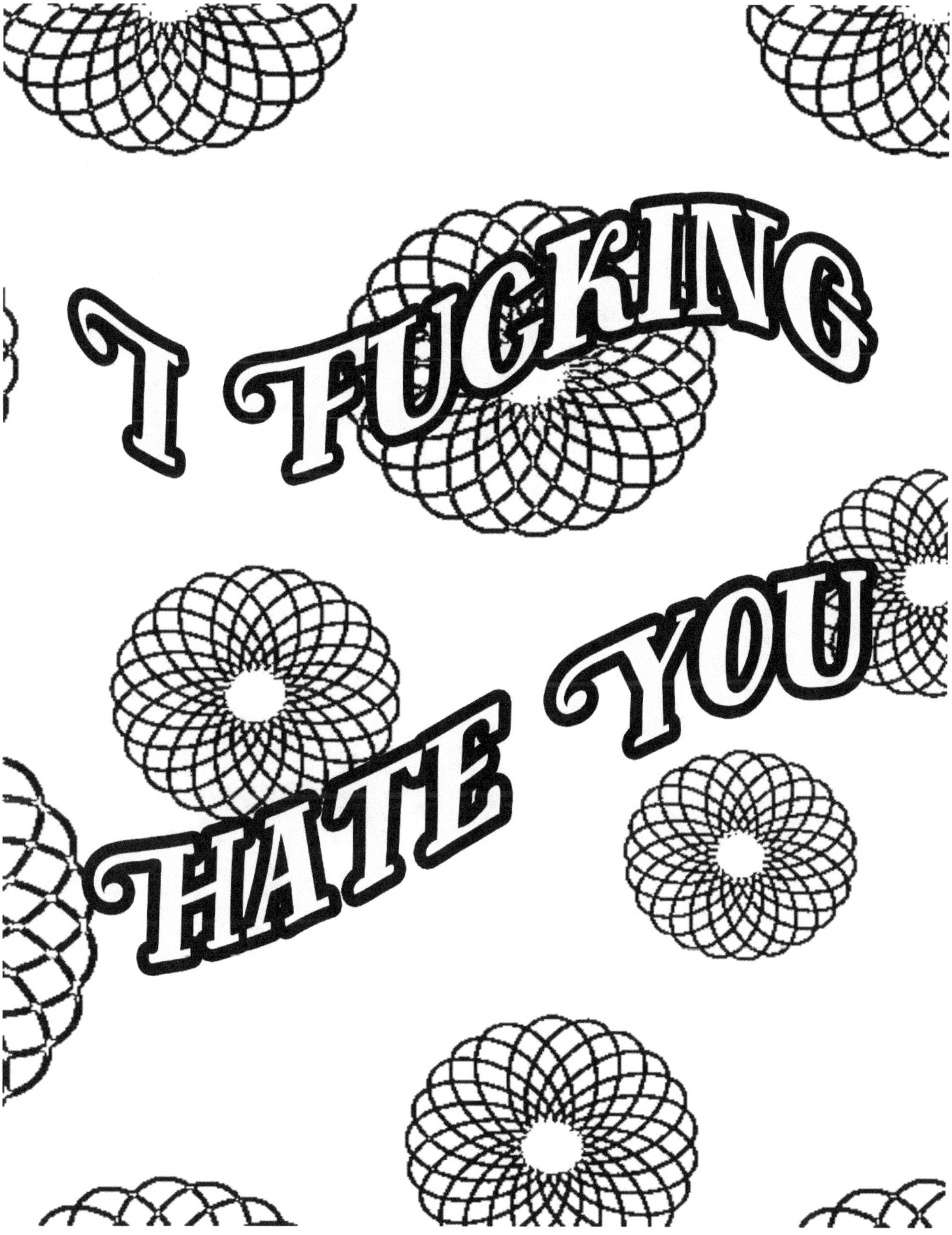
I FUCKING
HATE YOU

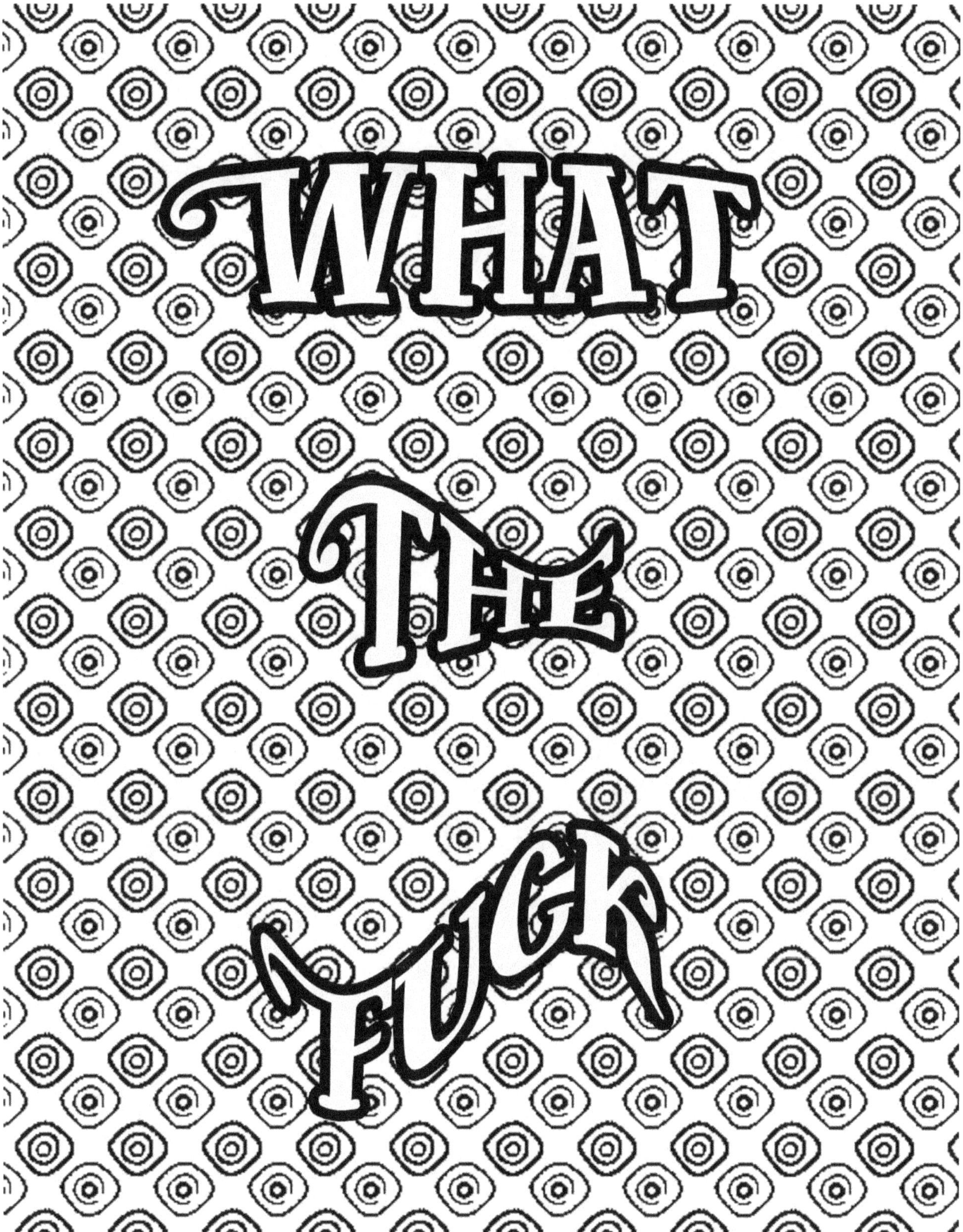
WHAT
THE
FUCK

SON OF

A BITCH

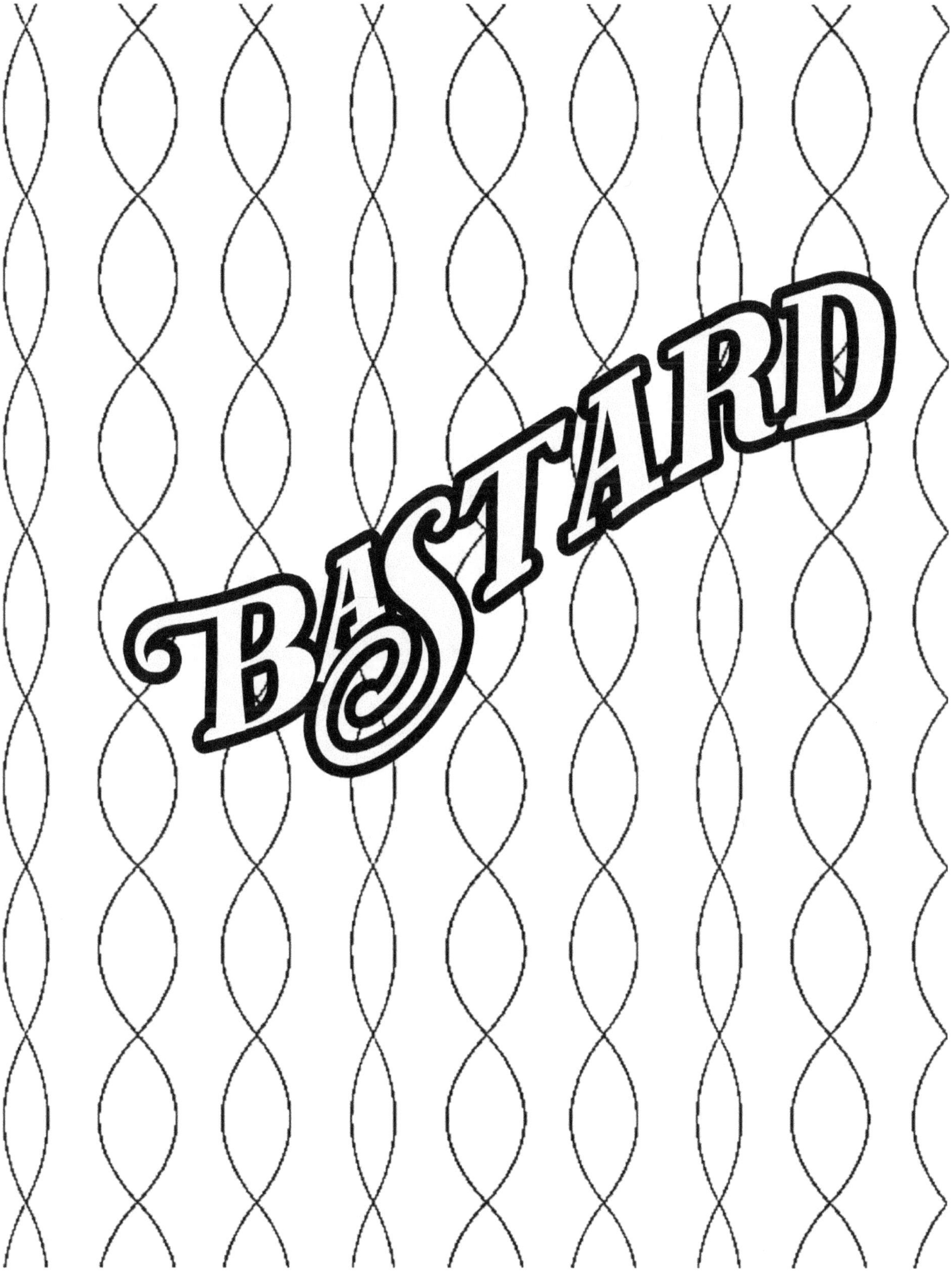
BASTARD

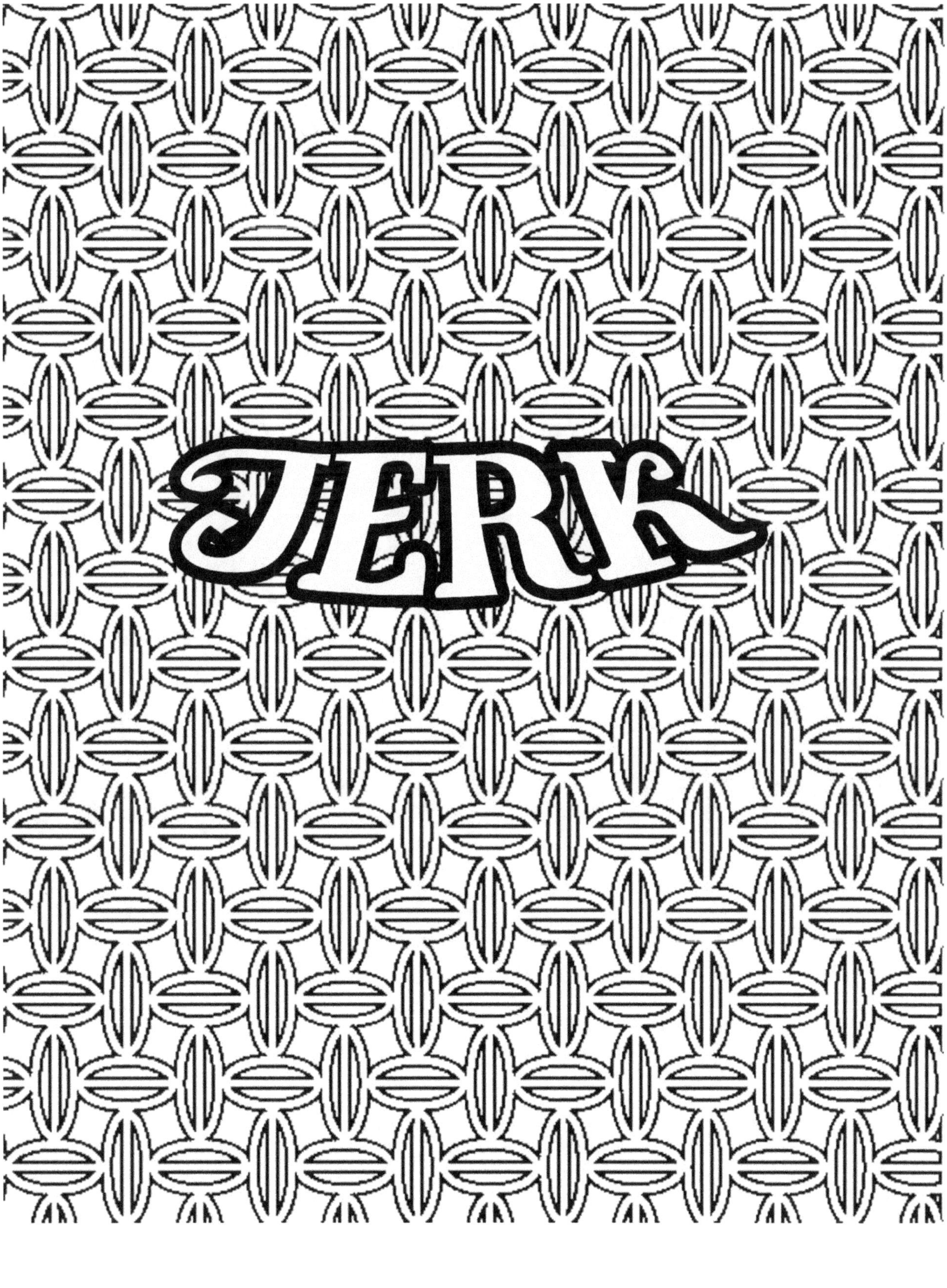
JERK

Note